TRUTHS
TO SPEAK
OVER YOURSELF

Rev Lori Skipper

Future Fire Mission
Copyright © 2012

TRUTHS TO SPEAK OVER YOURSELF

© 2012 Future Fire Mission
International Standard Book Number

Cover image by Rev Jerry Crow
Cover design by Rev Jerry Crow

All scripture quotations, unless otherwise indicated, are taken from the NEW KING JAMES VERSION ®. Copyright © 1982 by Thomas Nelson, Inc. Used by permission. All rights reserved.

Scripture quotations marked (AMP) are taken from the *Amplified Bible*, Copyright © 1954, 1958, 1962, 1964, 1965, 1987 by The Lockman Foundation. Used by permission.

Scripture quotations marked (NIV) are taken from the HOLY BIBLE, NEW INTERNATIONAL VERSION®. NIV ®. Copyright © 1973, 1978, 1984 by International Bible Society. Used by permission of Zondervan. All rights reserved.

Scripture quotations marked (KJV) are taken from the KING JAMES VERSION.

Strong's Exhaustive Concordance of the Bible by James Strong, Copyright © 1988 by Hendrickson Publishers, Peabody, Massachusetts. Used by permission. All rights reserved

ALL RIGHTS RESERVED.
No part of this publication may be reproduced, stored in a retrieval system, or transmitted, in any form or by any means – electronic, mechanical, photocopying, recording, or otherwise – without prior written permission of the publisher.

For information:
LORI SKIPPER
900 9TH AVE E LOT 211
PALMETTO, FL 34221
813-405-7854

Acknowledgements

First and foremost I would like to take this opportunity to express my deep love for my Lord and Savior Jesus Christ for giving me the Words that were necessary for me to even write this book. After all, He is the Word. I want to give glory to my heavenly Father for giving us the Word. For all Scripture is given by divine inspiration of God. I would also like to show my gratitude to Holy Spirit for giving me the unction to do this work. He has guided me through it all and for that I am eternally thankful.

I want to say thank you to my son Brad for giving me inspiration for the last 15 years. Brad, you are a wonderful young man and I am so very proud of you. Update: Brad is now 26 years old and has continued to be an inspiration to me. He has served our country as a US Marine.

To Brian, I can only hope and pray that one day we will be family again. I have missed you for the last 13 ½ years. You mean more to me than you will ever know. Update: Brian & I have reconciled our relationship. We met in March 2009 and have become extremely close. I cannot say thank you enough to the Father above for doing only what He could do in this situation.

To all my family and friends that have encouraged me and prayed for me through all my ups and downs. Those of you that have known me at my worst and that have seen me at my better. I can't say at my best because the best is yet to come. I truly appreciate all of you for believing in me when I did not believe in myself.

To you the reader, thank you for taking the time out of your busy schedule to spend a few minutes with me and for allowing Holy Spirit to speak to your spirit. May you be blessed as you take the TRUTHS found in this book and let them minister to your heart.

In Christ Love,

Rev. Lori Skipper

Foreword

Dear Readers,

It is a privilege for me to introduce Lori to you. Lori is what I would call a voice for God in these last days. I know that when you read this book, you are going to be taking in a part of Lori's heart. Nothing is as exciting to me as to know that, through this book, Lori is going to be reaching people she may never have the opportunity to meet in this life. I know that everyone who reads this book will want to meet the author. I assure you that the words of this book are very much a part of who she is. If you do not get the opportunity to meet her in person, you will have met her through her words. I pray that this book will be a blessing to you and that the words on the pages to follow will encourage, enlighten, and fill you to the uttermost in your spirit.

Thank you,

Rev Jerry Crow

Introduction

I came to write this book with the sole purpose of expressing my heart and sharing the Truths found in God's Word. I have a sordid past and with that it has brought me much shame and regrets. It took a long time for the Lord to wake me up to the Truth of what His Word says about me being washed white as snow. I, along with others that knew me, would remind me of who and what I used to be. The words you'll never amount to anything, you're fat, you're ugly, and you will never change used to ring through my head on a daily basis. It is only by Holy Spirit and the written Word of God that those words have been changed.

The Lord impressed upon my heart to write Truths To Speak Over Yourself about nine months ago. He had encouraged me with His word that says, "Call those things that aren't as though they were." So, that is what I began to do. I have noticed changes in my life since I began speaking God's Word over my life and my circumstances. Don't get me wrong, there are still times that my mouth runs too fast and I blurt out things that are reality and not Truth. But, praise the Lord, those times are getting fewer and farther between.

First order of business would be to make sure you have a saving relationship with Jesus Christ, as Lord and Savior. If you do not have that assurance please pray with me now, "Father, thank you for giving your Son Jesus for my sins. Jesus, I believe you died on a cross, rose from the dead and are seated in Heaven right now. I ask for forgiveness of all my sins and ask that You would come in to my heart right now. Thank You for this new life. I choose to live for You each and every day. In Jesus name, Amen & Amen."

It is my prayer that you will be changed as you begin to apply the Truths found in God's Word to your life. There are many Truths in the Word of God that you can speak over your life. I know there are many such books out there and I can only hope and pray that this one will be an added source of inspiration for you. Thank you for allowing me to come into your life and share with you the joys of being changed from glory to glory.

Truth to Speak Over Yourself:

"I have been given gifts by God and today I will walk in those gifts."

Devotion:

Have you ever sought the Lord and asked Him what gifts He has given to you? Have you ever thought I don't have any gifts? Unfortunately, there are many in the Body of Christ that believe that. I've heard, "God did not give me any gifts. I don't know what my gifts are. Gifts are only for Pastors or those in the ministry." None of these statements are correct. We are told in the Word of God "But the manifestation of the Spirit is given to each one for the profit of all: for to one is given the word of wisdom through the Spirit, to another the word of knowledge through the same Spirit, to another faith by the same Spirit, to another gifts of healings by the same spirit, to another the working of miracles, to another prophecy, to another discerning of spirits, to another different kinds of tongues, to another the interpretation of tongues. But one and the same Spirit works all these things, distributing to each one individually as He wills." This means that the Holy Spirit is responsible to give us the gifts. We are also told to desire spiritual gifts. If we are told these things, this must mean that all believers have gifts deposited in them. Jesus Himself walked in every gift listed in the Bible and since we have the Anointed One living in us, we must have gifts within us. These different gifts will manifest in our lives as the occasion calls for them. We have more prominent gifts and then those that the Holy Spirit anoints us with for the moment. I would like to exhort you just as Paul did with Timothy, "stir up the gift that is within you." It is our responsibility to stir up the gifts. Remember, just as Jesus lives within us, so do the gifts given by the Holy Spirit.

1 Corinthians 12:7-10; 2 Timothy 1:6; 1 Corinthians 14:1

Truth to Speak Over Yourself:

"My children are faithful to study the Word and they walk with the Lord daily."

Devotion:

How many of us have children and see them doing things that we know are going to cause them pain? We would do just about anything if we could direct them to go another direction. Instead of us repeating over and over the things that they are doing wrong, let's focus on what the Word of God tells us today. In Isaiah 54:13, we are told that the Lord will teach our children. Who could ask for a better teacher? We are also told if we, as parents, train our children in the way they should go they will not depart from it when they are older. Even if we made mistakes or did not serve Jesus Christ when they were younger, our children still learn the Truth when we come to a saving relationship with Him. As we teach them, in both word and deed, and they attend church services with us, they are learning the Word of God. The Word of God is powerful and The Truth and if it says the Lord will teach them, He will. So instead of us focusing on the mistakes we think they are making, let us focus on their areas of strength and thank the Lord today that they are making right choices according to His Word. As we continue to confess this truth over our children, their choices will begin to line up with the Word of God and not necessarily our desires for them.

Isaiah 54:13; Proverbs 22:6

Truth to Speak Over Yourself:

"I submit myself to the Lord, resist the devil and he has to flee."

Devotion:

We are told in Ephesians 4:27 (AMP) "Leave no [such] room *or* foothold for the devil [give no opportunity to him]." Too many times we allow the devil to have a room or foothold in our lives. We do this by having bad attitudes, anger, bitterness, jealousy, unforgiveness, etc. When we seek to have our own way instead of walking in the way the Lord has directed us, we have given Satan legal access. We have walked in disobedience and rebellion. The Word of God tells us that rebellion is the same as divination (witchcraft). There are so many in the Body of Christ that are attempting to resist the devil but they have ignored the first part of James 4:7. We must first submit ourselves to God, and then resist the devil, and then he will flee. Let's get the first part down pat first. To submit to God means letting Him be Lord over our lives. It means letting Him have control over our lives. It means saying 'yes' to His ways and 'no' to ours. Once we do this, on a consistent basis, then we can resist the devil, and he has to flee. Are you being harassed today and not sure if you've opened the door to the devil? Take time today to submit (surrender) to God, resist the devil, and watch him flee.

Ephesians 4:27 (AMP); James 4:7; and 1 Samuel 15:23

Truth to Speak Over Yourself:

"I can do all things through Christ who strengthens me."

Devotion:

In January 2006, one of the members from the church I attended lost his nine-year-old daughter. She was killed in an auto accident with her mother. That same week, a wife lost her husband at the age of 46 years old. The man that lost his daughter came to a revival service that our church was holding two days after her death. I was amazed at the strength that he exhibited. He has continued to come to every church service and has shown great strength and joy since that time. He has used his tragedy to help others in their grief and there have been many that have come to know Jesus through his testimony. I have only met the woman that lost her husband one time. I was very impressed by her though. A week after she lost her husband, she came into a McDonalds were I was at and spoke to the woman that I was with. She made a very profound comment and I'd like to share it. She said, "He's dead and I have a choice to make. I can both lie down and die or I can live. And I choose to live." She gave all the credit for her strength to Jesus Christ. She knows that it is only through Him and by Him that she is walking strong. I would like to make a point here; both of these people know Jesus Christ and trust Him to carry them through. They are both also using their personal tragedies to witness for Christ. When we go through trying times, we need to remember that our testimonies are to be used for God's glory and to bring comfort to others.

Philippians 4:13

Truth to Speak Over Yourself:

"In all things I seek first the kingdom of God and His righteousness; therefore, all these things will be added unto me."

Devotion:

What are you lacking in your life today? Are you short on finances, joy, health, friends, or peace? Whatever you find yourself in need of today, the Word of God gives us the answer. So many times I catch myself seeking after those things that are lacking in my life instead of obeying Gods Word. He said in Matthew 6:33 (KJV), "Seek ye first the kingdom of God and His righteousness and all these will be added unto you." I'm reminded of Solomon. When God told him to ask for anything he wanted and he'd receive it, Solomon asked for wisdom and knowledge to lead the people. God was pleased with Solomon's request and gave him all things abundantly. Jesus is wisdom so if we will obey God's Word and seek His kingdom and His righteousness first, we too will receive all things abundantly. The most important thing that we receive is spiritual blessings. As we continue to grow spiritually, the natural wants and needs that we have will not seem as large as they once did. As we know that all things will be added unto us, we need to remember that the timing is the Lord's. We will receive all that we have need of in His timing, not our own. We need to learn to trust in His perfect timing. God is a God of order so we need to put things in order. First means before anything else. Today, before you begin to worry about any lack you may have, seek the kingdom of God and His righteousness. When we do this first, the rest does not seem as big or as bad as it once did.

Matthew 6:33 (KJV); 2 Chronicles 1:10-12

Truth to Speak Over Yourself:

"I guard my mouth from murmuring and complaining."

Devotion:

There is a saying that has been around for a while now. The saying goes something like this, "all God's children have trouble." There is so much truth to that saying. There is not one person on the face of this earth that does not have trials and tribulations. Whether we are children of God or not yet born again, we have troubles. We all have a choice to make. I know that it seems easier to grumble and complain over the things we are going through but when this is the choice we make, we stay in that mess. I know from personal experience that when I grumble and complain over my situation, depression begins to grab on. When depression grabs on, my body begins to hurt and my attitude begins to stink. But, when I choose to offer up a sacrifice of praise and thanksgiving, the joy of the Lord begins to flood me. As the joy of the Lord floods me, the manifest presence of the Lord comes and there is no pain, worry, or distress. If I stay in a mode of grumbling and complaining, the troubles begin to get bigger and I begin to feel as if I'm going under. When I choose to guard my mouth and tongue from grumbling and complaining, my whole outlook is better. The situation may not actually be any better, but my attitude is. The next time the temptation to grumble and complain comes over you, make the choice to offer up a sacrifice of praise and thanksgiving and notice the whole atmosphere change.

Proverbs 13:3; Hebrews 13:15

Truth to Speak Over Yourself:

"My husband is the head of our household and I will respect and honor him."

Devotion:

Ladies- our husbands need encouragement. I was having a conversation with my best friend one day about our spouses. We both had questions and concerns so we did the best thing we could do, we prayed. As we were praying, I began to thank God for creating men and women differently. I thanked Him for making men physically stronger than women, for making men the head of the households, the protectors, the providers, and the disciplinarian. Then I began to thank Him for creating women to be submissive to their husbands, for making us weaker physically, and for making us stronger in other areas than men are. If our husbands are making decisions that we are not in agreement with, we need to be praying for them, not nagging them. We need to encourage them and let them know how much we appreciate all that they do for our marriage and homes. We are told in Ephesians 5:33 (AMP), "However, let each man of you [without exception] love his wife as [being in a sense] his very own self; and let the wife see that she respects *and* reverences her husband [that she notices him, regards him, honors him, prefers him, venerates, and esteems him; and that she defers to him, praises him, and loves and admires him exceedingly]." Nowhere in this verse does it say that we are to respect him only when he deserves or earns it. If we will begin to recognize our husbands' strengths and not only point out their weaknesses, they will begin to feel better about themselves. When they feel better about themselves, we will reap the benefits. This is an area that I must daily pray about for myself. My husband and I are definitely different in areas of our lives and this can be a good thing or a trying matter. I do not want to mistreat my husband with my words so I must pray for God to change me and help me to be an encouragement to him and not a hindrance. If we just point out the areas that we don't agree with, they will become defeated and stop doing anything to help us, so we need to praise them and encourage them in every area of their lives. As we pray and ask the Lord to change us and we allow those changes to happen, our husbands will begin to respond to the changes in us and they too will change.

Proverbs 31:10-12; Revelation 1:6 (KJV); Proverbs 21:1; Ephesians 5:33 (AMP)

Truth to Speak Over Yourself:

"In this world there will be tribulation, but I will be of good cheer, for Christ Jesus has overcome the world."

Devotion:

My whole walk with the Lord He has always given me themes to live by. The newest theme for me is, "There will be trouble, trials, and tribulation in this world". You see, even though we are born again and living in the Spirit, we still live in a sin sick world and have a fleshly tent that we live in. When trouble comes, we're not exempt from it just because we are children of God. We are also told in 1 Corinthians 10:13 (AMP) "For no temptation (no trial regarded as enticing to sin, no matter how it comes or where it leads) has overtaken you *and* laid hold on you that is not common to man [that is, no temptation or trial has come to you that is beyond human resistance and that is not adjusted and adapted and belonging to human experience, and such as man can bear.] But God is faithful [to His Word and to His compassionate nature], and He [can be trusted] not to let you be tempted *and* tried *and* assayed beyond your ability *and* strength of resistance *and* power to endure, but with the temptation He will [always] also provide the way out (the means of escape to a landing place), that you may be capable *and* strong *and* powerful to bear up under it patiently." But, we can be in good cheer when it comes our way (and it will) because Jesus overcame the world with His death and resurrection. The world is watching us and they see what we're going through but more importantly, they are watching how we go through the tribulation, trials, and trouble. What do they see when they look at you? Do they see gloom, doom, and doubt? Or do they see peace, joy, and good cheer? If they see the gloom and doom, repent and ask God to once again give you His peace and good cheer. May you always remember that Jesus has overcome the world and this is only our temporary home.

John 16:33; 1 Corinthians 10:13 (AMP)

Truth to Speak Over Yourself:

"I bring every thought into obedience to Christ Jesus."

Devotion:

"Satan is a liar and the father of lies." "The thief does not come except to steal, kill, and destroy." One of the number one ways that he attempts to steal, kill, and destroy is through our thought life. When we are in the midst of a battle, which seems easier to do; think on the battle or the Word of God? If we are honest with ourselves, we think more on the battle than on the Word of God. We are told in God's Word to "cast down arguments and every high thing that exalts itself against the knowledge of God, bringing every thought into captivity to the obedience of Christ," When Satan attacks our minds with thoughts of failure, impossibilities, strife, and fear and we do not cast them down, we are allowing the thief to steal our joy, kill our hope, and destroy our faith. We are also told in the Word of God that we are not unaware of Satan's devices. That means that he does not change his tactics. He has been using the same ones for years now and we should be aware of (familiar with) them. When we recognize one of the enemy's tactics being brought against us, we need to remind him that he is a liar and the father of lies and then remind him of the Word of God. For it is written: we are not unaware of your schemes and we take every thought captive and into obedience to Jesus Christ in Jesus name. Whether we are having positive or negative thoughts, let us remember to bring every one of them into captivity to the obedience of Jesus Christ. As we continue to allow the Word of God to penetrate our minds, we will continue to walk in the victory that Jesus Christ provided for us.

John 8:44; 2 Corinthians 2:11; 2 Corinthians 10:5; John 10:10

Truth to Speak Over Yourself:

"I have purposed that my mouth will not transgress, but I will speak praises of the Lord all day long."

Devotion:

I don't know about you, but my mouth can get me into trouble sometimes. In today's 'Truth to Speak Over Yourself' we see the word transgress. The word transgress in the Hebrew is abar (aw-bar'). This word means to cross over, to cover, alienate, alter, meddle, overrun, provoke to anger, perish, and turn away. These are just a few of the meanings of that one word transgress. When we read in Psalm 17:3 b (KJV) "I am purposed that my mouth shall not transgress", this tells us that we have a choice to make. Will we cross over, alienate, meddle, or provoke to anger? Or will we speak blessings, righteousness and praise of God? In the NIV of Psalm 17:3 b we read the word sin instead of transgress. When we allow ourselves to meddle and cross over, we are walking in sin. Psalm 35:38 (NIV) tell us "My tongue will speak of Your righteousness and of Your praises all day long." Again we see we have a choice. My tongue will speak of His righteousness or it will speak of my failures. When we allow ourselves to gossip, backbite, slander, or meddle in other people's business, we are transgressing and not speaking forth the praises of God. God created man in His image and in His likeness and when we put people down it is the same thing as putting God down. So, let us purpose (choose) not to transgress today and purpose (choose) to speak forth the righteousness and praises of God all day long.

Psalm 17:3 (KJV & NIV); Psalm 35:8 (NIV) (Hebrew definition taken from Strong's Exhaustive Concordance)

Truth to Speak Over Yourself:

"By Jesus stripes I am healed!"

Devotion:

In June 1996 a train hit me. I fractured my neck in two places, broke my tailbone and had numerous bruises covering my body. Since that time and until recently I had been in horrible pain daily. At that time I did not know Jesus Christ so I did not know that I could even pray against the pain. As a result of the train accident, I had chronic degenerative disc disease with several herniated and bulging discs in both my neck and back. I also had lupus and fibromyalgia. Since coming to know Christ as my personal Lord and Savior, He has healed me of TMJ, dislocated kneecap, lupus, depression and now fibromyalgia and degenerative disc disease. Others and I have prayed daily for the manifestation of the healing Jesus provided for me. On April 14, 2006, I received the miracles of the release of the chronic pain in my body. I have had five pain free days and that is a miracle. I have confessed for years that I was healed by Jesus stripes. I knew that I was already healed and that I was just experiencing symptoms. But, those symptoms do not have any right to come against our bodies or minds because Jesus took the beatings so we do not have to suffer from sickness, pain, or disease. When Jesus went to the cross, He took everything upon Himself and said, "It is finished!" It is time for us to believe in our hearts, not just mentally, that Jesus truly took it all so that we can be healed. When we gave our hearts to the Lord and became new creations in Christ Jesus, we were healed. The next time pain, sickness, or depression tries to come upon your body or mind, remind Jesus, Satan, and yourself that by Jesus stripes you are healed. Don't confess that you are sick, confess that you have symptoms but by His stripes you are healed. Do not accept anything less than what God says is yours. Reality may say you have pain but the TRUTH is you are healed.

Isaiah 53:3-4; 1 Peter 2:24; 2 Corinthians 5:17

Truth to Speak Over Yourself:

"I lay hands on the sick, and they recover."

Devotion:

We are told in Mark 16:17-18, "And these signs will follow those who believe: In My name they will cast out demons; they will speak with new tongues; they will take up serpents; and if they drink anything deadly, it will by no means hurt them; they will lay hands on the sick, and they will recover." This says that those who believe. Is Jesus saying those who believe in Him or those who believe the signs will follow them? I believe that it is referring to both. There are many believers today who do not believe these signs are for today and that they went out with the early apostles. Then there are believers who do not believe that these signs will follow them and guess what? They don't. I, for one, believe that these signs do follow me and I have had the pleasure of personally experiencing them and operating in them. Now, don't get me wrong, I am first a believer in Jesus Christ. I do not operate in the signs for myself, but for those who need to be set free and to build the Kingdom of God. If we are walking in doubt that any of the mentioned gifts will operate in and through us, they won't. How many times do we personally have a sickness or pain try to come upon our bodies and we do not do anything about it, or we wait for someone else to pray for us? We have the power in us to lay hands on ourselves and to see ourselves healed. We would be doing well to believe the Whole Word of God and to take God at His Word. It is our responsibility to be obedient to the Lord and it is His responsibility to perform His Word.

Mark 16:17-18

Truth to Speak Over Yourself:

"I daily study the Word of God."

Devotion:

We are told in 2 Timothy 2:15 (AMP) "Study *and* be eager *and* do your utmost to present yourself to God approved (tested by trial), a workman who has no cause to be ashamed, correctly analyzing *and* accurately dividing [rightly handling and skillfully teaching] the Word of Truth." In the NKJV, it says to "be diligent in presenting ourselves to God." Paul told Timothy in 1 Timothy 4:13 "Till I come, give attention to reading, to exhortation, to doctrine." That same word applies to our own lives today. We are being shown through these Scriptures how important it is to study the Word of God. Not only should we read the Word but study it. There are so many people today that want to play Russian roulette with the Word of God. There are also those that want to interpret the Word to fit what they want it to mean. That is why I like the Amplified Version, for it says to correctly analyze and correctly divide the Word of Truth. The Word of God is God Himself speaking to us. He inspired men to write the words but the Words are God's words. The reason we want to study the Word and be diligent in doing so is that we may present ourselves to God, a workman that need not be ashamed. I don't know about you, but I do not want to be ashamed when I approach God in prayer or when I stand before Him on Judgment Day. I want to rightly handle and teach the Word of God. In order for us to know God and to know His will for us and for others is to study the Word. Now I'm not talking about religion that says you must or have to read the Word but I'm talking about freedom and relationship that says we get to read and study the Word of God. I have heard it said that the Bible is our road map, guidebook, and basic instructions before leaving earth and to all these sayings I say Amen. Let the Word of God guide and direct you today. Make a new commitment today to study the Word of God and allow the Holy Spirit to enlighten you to the Truths within it.

2 Timothy 2:15 (AMP & NKJV); 1 Timothy 4:13

Truth to Speak Over Yourself:

"I am not just a hearer of the Word but am a doer of the Word as well."

Devotion:

"What do you mean be a doer of the Word?" We are told in James 1:22 "But be doers of the Word, and not hearers only, deceiving yourselves." The Word of God is our road map to life. If we read, hear, and study the Word but do not do the Word, we are just getting head knowledge. The way for something to take hold in our lives is to put that something into action. If we were to go on a trip to a place we've never been, we would need directions and possibly a map. If someone were to give us the directions and we bought a map but never looked at the map or followed the directions, how far do you think we would make it? Not far, or at least probably not in the right direction. Unfortunately, there are many in the Body of Christ today that do that same thing with the Word of God. Some never even open it and then there are those that do read it but never do it. Because we sometimes read the Word but do not apply the Word, we just keep going around and around in circles. We just read in James that if we are not doers but hearers only, we deceive ourselves. It does not say that someone else is deceiving us but we ourselves. I would have to say a big "Ouch!" to that one. I've been guilty, how about you? The last part of our truth is that we meditate on the Word all the day long. We will find ourselves through the day meditating on something and the best thing we can meditate on is the written Word of God. As we meditate on the Word, it will get down deep into our heart and change us. As we allow the Word into our heart, it will prevent us from sinning. How do we know if we are about to sin? By knowing God and His Word. His Word will guide and direct us, if we will allow it to. I pray that today you will be free as you meditate on God's Word and then become a doer of the Word.

James 1:22; Psalm 1:2; Psalm 119:11

Truth to Speak Over Yourself

"I take care of my body which is the temple of the Holy Ghost."

Devotion:

Have you accepted Jesus Christ as your Lord and Savior? If the answer is yes to that question, then your body is now the Holy Spirit's temple. You see, when we get born again; we are indwelt with the Holy Spirit. That means to say, we become His abode. He comes to live in us. This is different than the baptism of the Holy Spirit. Since the Holy Spirit lives in us and directs our lives, as well as interceding for us, shouldn't we be careful of what we put in our bodies? I had smoked for 20 some odd years and still smoked for 2 years after I got born again. In February of 1999, I knew that it was time to quit smoking because the conviction was so strong. At this time, the Lord revealed to me that the Holy Spirit lives in me and that I was basically causing Him to smoke because of my actions. Don't get me wrong, I'm not coming down on anyone who smokes, I'm just letting you know what the Lord revealed to me. We need to get a revelation of being the temple of the Holy Spirit. When we indulge ourselves in over-eating, not resting enough, watching the wrong stuff on television or the net, or read the wrong materials, we are subjecting the Holy Spirit to those same practices. He is a God who is without sin and He does not want any part of our sins. We have this mindset that says, "What I do with my body won't harm anyone," but it will. Some of our actions will grieve the Holy Spirit and bring harm to ourselves and we are the temples of the Holy Spirit; therefore bringing harm to Him. If you take part in any of the above mentioned activities or any other that would affect your body, like over-working, sleeping to much, etc. maybe this would be a good time to go before the Lord, and ask for His help so that you may become a clean and healthy temple for the Holy Spirit to live in.

1 Corinthians 6:19-20

Truth to Speak Over Yourself

"I am a giver. I work to make a giving, not a living."

Devotion:

One of the reasons the Lord blesses us is so we can bless someone else. We are told in 2 Corinthians 9:7-8 "So let each one give as he purposes in his heart, not grudgingly or of necessity, for God loves a cheerful giver. And God is able to make all grace abound toward you, that you, always having all sufficiency in all things, may have an abundance for every good work." The principle in this Scripture is we give out of a cheerful and willing heart, and then God will ensure that we have all sufficiency in all things. Did you notice the word all? Do you know what that means? If you said all or everything, you were right. There have been times that I knew the Lord had asked me to give to someone and I barely had enough to cover my needs, but I gave and He blessed me in return. Then there were times that He asked me to give and I purposed in my heart what I was going to give but when the time came, I began to waiver and even did so grudgingly. Those times, I did not reap such a great blessing. I have learned to understand what Jesus meant when He said, "It is more blessed to give, than to receive." When I see people hurting and not being able to do the things that are needful and I can help, I get blessed just by being able to help them. I am not only talking about helping financially. I have not always been able to help financially but I can help in other ways, such as: mowing the lawn, shoveling the walk, lending an ear, praying, or finding other people that can help. There are many ways that a person can give if we would just take the time to look and pray. God loves to bless His people so that we can be a blessing to others and this does not mean just born again believers. God wants us to bless those that do not yet have a relationship with Him so we can witness to them. Begin to ask the Lord to cause you to be a distribution center for Him and He will do it. Follow the principles in His Word and the promises will come to pass.

Acts 20:35; 2 Corinthians 9:7-8

Truth to Speak Over Yourself

"I prosper in everything I put my hand to."

Devotion:

I'd like to share with you the Hebrew meanings of prosper, found in the Strong's Exhaustive Concordance. Prosper: To push forward in various forms-break out, come (mightily), go over, be good, be meet, be profitable, (cause to, effect, make to, send) prosper (-ity, -ous, -ously.) The word prosper in the Greek means to help on the road, i.e. (pass) succeed in reaching; fig. to succeed in business affairs:-(have a) prosper (-ous journey). As you can see, prosperity is a good thing. We are called to prosper in every area of our lives, spiritually, financially, mentally, and socially. We need to keep it in the correct order though and seek after spiritual prosperity first. In 3 John 2 (AMP) we read "Beloved, I pray that you may prosper in every way and [that your body] may keep well, even as [I know] your soul keeps well *and* prospers." The only way we will prosper in every way, including the prosperity of our body, is when our soul prospers first. Now, this is not talking of our will, mind, and emotions, this is speaking of our spirit man. As our spirit man prospers and we grow in the knowledge of Jesus Christ, our will, mind, and emotions will prosper. We can also tell by the meaning of the word prosper; one of the reasons we prosper is so we may cause others to prosper. In Joshua 1:8 it is we that make our way prosperous. We expect God to do everything and if you will ponder on that for just a moment, you will see that He already has done everything for us. We read in Joshua 1:8 that if we will meditate on the Word day and night and observe and do all that is written in it, then we will make our way prosperous and have good success. We will make our way prosperous, which sounds to me as if the responsibility is on our part. There are so many today that are afraid of responsibility but it really is a good thing, because as we do our part and meditate on the Word, and become doers of the Word, God will do His part and see that we prosper in all areas of our lives. Are you struggling financially, physically, spiritually, or mentally today? Begin to meditate on and do the Word and remind God of His Word and watch the Word work. It is my prayer that 3 John 2 will come to pass in your life beginning today.

Genesis 39:3; Joshua 1:8 (AMP); 3 John 2 (AMP) (Hebrew and Greek meanings taken from Strong's Exhaustive Concordance)

Truth to Speak Over Yourself

"I know that in all things God works for the good of me because I love Him and am the called according to His purpose."

Devotion:

I know that some really horrible things happen to us sometimes. I also know that sometimes we do not understand why we are going through what we are at the time. There is one thing that we can be sure of in the midst of the tough times and that is; "We are assured *and* know that [God being a partner in their labor] all things work together *and* are [fitting into a plan] for good to *and* for those who love God and are called according to [His] design and purpose." Romans 8:28 (AMP) We only see a small portion of the picture but God, in His infinite wisdom, sees the whole picture and knows every little detail of what we are going through and what the end result is going to be. Think back to Joseph, his own brothers sold him into slavery, Potiphar's wife lied on him, he was thrown into prison, but the end result was reconciliation with his family and provision in great abundance. I'm sure that in the beginning of his trial, he could not see where any of this would work out for his good but he continued to trust God in every situation that he went through and he came out victoriously. I have gone through some things in my life that would cause quite a few people to turn their backs on the Lord or at the very least become bitter, but I have chosen to keep my eyes fixed on Jesus, allow Him to heal me, allow Him to work His forgiveness in and through my life, and allow His love to flow through me and I have come out victoriously. If you would allow me to, I would like to pray with you. Father, in the name of Jesus, whatever my dear brother or sister is going through this day, I ask that You would manifest Your presence and power in their life right now. I ask that they would experience Your love in a brand new way today. I pray for peace and joy to come upon them. I pray for Your strength to carry through to the very end. Where there needs to be healing, I ask for their healing and where there is bondage, I ask for Your deliverance. I cancel every demonic spirit that is operating in their life and I ask for You to fill them to overflowing with Your Spirit. Lord, we don't understand why we go through some of the things we go through, but we choose right now to keep our eyes fixed on Jesus and we choose to trust You that all things will work together for our good. Help them to understand that they do not walk alone, but You are with them every moment of every day. Lord, we love You and worship You for Who You are and for what You are doing in our lives. May You be glorified in our lives this day. In Jesus name, amen and amen. I pray that you will prosper in everything you put your hand to today.

Romans 8:28 (AMP); Genesis 37, 39, and 45

Truth to Speak Over Yourself:

"I will teach the Word of God and will remain teachable today."

Devotion:

For those of us that are adults, let's think back a moment to our childhood. When we were in school, how many of us really enjoyed being taught? Or when our parent's tried to teach us rules, did we enjoy that? So many times, we balk at others trying to teach us but if we want to teach others, we must first be taught. I have a saying that speaks volumes to me, "I can only give out what I have in me and I don't want to give myself out. I want to give out Jesus." Therefore, I must be taught by Jesus and those He has put in charge of teaching me. If I do not have it in me, I cannot give it out. There is not one of us that know everything there is to know about any area of life. When we are employed, we must continually be learning and growing in our knowledge of our job in order to be an asset to our employer. As we continue to serve Jesus Christ, we must continue to learn and grow in our knowledge of Him in order to be an asset to our King. God is looking for those that are going to work with Him to expand His Kingdom, and to do so effectively we must learn His will and His ways. We read in 2 Timothy 2:24, "And a servant of the Lord must not quarrel but be gentle to all, able to teach, patient," and Titus 1:9 tells us, "holding fast the faithful word as he has been taught, that he may be able, by sound doctrine, both to exhort and convict those who contradict." There are principles found in these Scriptures, we must be taught first, remember what we've been taught; then and only then, can we teach others. I would like to make another point here, our children are watching us and learning what they are seeing, so what are we teaching them by our actions? The next time someone starts to tell us something that we 'think' we already know, why don't we be still long enough for them to tell us what they know and we just might learn something. May God open your heart and ears to hear what the Spirit is saying.

2 Timothy 2:24; Titus 1:9

Truth to Speak Over Yourself

"I have been forgiven much so I will forgive much."

Devotion:

We have many opportunities in this life to hate someone. We have horrible things that we go through and most of it is caused by people. The Lord tells us that if we do not forgive others, we ourselves will not be forgiven. One of the ways that I find it easier to forgive someone when they have wronged me or flat out hurt me, is to remember that I wronged and hurt Jesus yet He forgave me of all my sins. There is not one person that has ever done to me the horrible things that others did to Jesus. Yet, when He hung on the Cross, He said to our Father in Heaven, "Forgive them, for they know not what they do." He was talking about those that hung Him on the Cross after beating Him and putting a crown of thorns on His head. He was also talking about you and me and all those that have been born since that time. I have been abused and mistreated in my life but never to the point that Jesus went through. We are also told in the Word of God that if you hate in your heart, you are the same as a murderer. These are hard words to swallow but they are the truth! 1 John 2:11 tells us: "But he who hates his brother is in darkness and walks in darkness, and does not know where he is going, because the darkness has blinded his eyes." When we became new creatures in Christ Jesus, we were translated from darkness and placed into God's glorious light. Darkness is where Satan lives. If you claim to walk with Jesus, then you must, according to the Word of God, walk in the light. I had spent years of having unforgiveness in my life and I was miserable. I did not realize how much unforgiveness I had but once the Lord revealed it and I chose to forgive those that had hurt me, I instantly felt better physically, mentally, and spiritually. We all have emotions but we do not have to allow the emotions to control us but instead, let us control our emotions. Let me leave you with this Word: "And be kind to one another, tenderhearted, forgiving one another, even as God in Christ forgave you."

1 John 2:11; Ephesians 4:32; 1 John 3:15; Matthew 6:14; Luke 23:34

Truth to Speak Over Yourself

"I am strong and courageous. I am not terrified; nor discouraged. The Lord my God is with me wherever I go."

Devotion:

We are promised numerous times in the Word of God that God Himself is with us. He has promised to never leave us nor forsake us, which means He will not abandon us. As I have walked this journey with Him, He has proven time and time again that He really is with me. One of the names of our God is Jehovah Rohi, which means the Lord Who Sees. When Abraham and Sarah sent Hagar away, she found herself in the wilderness with her son Ishmael, out of water and out of strength. It was at this time that she began to cry aloud to herself. But much to her surprise, God was there. She soon discovered that although she felt alone she was never really alone. No matter what we face in this life, we are never alone. If we are walking with God, or if we are far from Him, He is always there, watching. In the beginning of my walk with Him, I came to find out that my life verse was found in Joshua 1:9. "Have I not commanded you? Be strong and of good courage; do not be afraid, nor be dismayed, for the Lord your God is with you wherever you go." I have held on to this Scripture as an anchor. When it seemed as if all Hell had been loosed against me, I would hear the promise of God that He is with me. I would like to leave with you an encouraging word to help you through the battle that you face today. "Teaching them to observe all things that I have commanded you; and lo, I am with you always, even to the end of the age." Amen.

Genesis 21:8-21; Joshua 1:9; Matthew 28:20; Hebrews 13:5

Truth to Speak Over Yourself

"I cast all my care on the Lord for He cares for me."

Devotion:

How many of us are called worrywarts? According to the Word of God, we are not to worry. We think that our problems are either too small or too big for us to release to God. We have this mental picture that we must take care of everything ourselves. Why should we bother God with our problems, after all, He has so much else to take care of, what with the wars and all. We are told in the Word, to cast all of our cares upon the Lord, for He cares for us. Do you have a problem casting all of your cares on Him? Do you have a problem believing that He cares for you? The word cast in the original Greek language means: to throw upon; to fling. If you have ever gone fishing, you know that when you cast out, you must cast fairly hard. If you cast softly, the line will just drop in front of you. God does not want us to cast softly and have all of our cares just drop in front of us. He knows that if they are just lying at our feet, we will pick them up again. If we will throw or fling them upon God, they will go the distance and be out of our reach. I want you to notice that He says _all_ our cares. He does not just want the ones that really bog us down, but all of them. As I've been walking through another trial recently, I thought that I was doing really well at not picking up the burden and letting the Lord take care of my cares. But I was wrong, I began to have physical symptoms of pain and fatigue and it wasn't until I was at church a few days ago that I realized I hadn't really cast all of my cares upon the Lord. As I began to literally fling them upon Him, I felt better almost instantly. Are you experiencing pain, fatigue, or depression? If so, ask the Holy Spirit to reveal to you if you have been holding onto your cares instead of casting them on to the Lord. If He reveals any areas in your life, then fling them over onto the Lord, for He really does care for you.

1 Peter 5:7 (Greek meanings taken from Strong's Exhaustive Concordance)

Truth to Speak Over Yourself

"My children shall live long, prosperous lives because they honor and obey their parents."

Devotion:

My son is currently 15 years old. I hear the groans and the ahhhs. You know what I'm talking about before I even say any more. But honestly, I am blessed. I have a son that is walking with the Lord and has almost always been very well behaved. My son definitely has his own personality, although at times, he reminds me so much of myself, that it is hard to discipline him when it is needed. My son has a very unique sense of humor. He can crack me up without even trying, except for the times he's trying to be funny when he should be being serious, like when he's getting reprimanded. One of the greatest gifts that the Lord has given to my son is wisdom. He gave his life to Jesus Christ as a seven year old and has been walking with Him since. There have been times that it would have been easier to go with the crowd and do what they wanted but he has walked in the wisdom and discipline of the Lord. My son is very independent and likes to do things his way. And at times, this has been an area of difficulty for him because he cannot always do things his way. It is at these times that I could just about scream, well; maybe I did once in a while. But, this does not mean he is rebellious, just his own person. As a young child, he would go through his toys and give them to less fortunate children. He would also give his money to others that had a need (this he still does). We need to remember that children are a blessing from God. Instead of us parents focusing so much on the things that our children do that we don't like, it's time we focus on the good things that our children do and give them praise for it. Now, I'm not talking about the praise we give to the Lord but our children need to hear that we are proud of them and that they did a good job. We read in Ephesians 6:1-3 "Children, obey your parents in the Lord, for this is right. Honor your father and mother, which is the first commandment with promise: "that it may go well with you and you may live long on the earth." This does not say that our children should honor us because we deserve it but so that they may live a long good life. In Proverbs 16:16 we read about getting wisdom and understanding. If your child is strong-willed and stubborn, instead of repeating that over and over and calling them rebellious, begin to speak a blessing over them and begin to pray the Word of God over them, then watch the transformation in front of your very eyes.

Ephesians 6:1-3; Proverbs 16:16

Truth to Speak Over Yourself

"I was born to fellowship with Jesus."

Devotion:

"Be unceasing in prayer [praying perseveringly]." You may be wondering, "How can I possibly pray without ceasing?" When you became born again, your spirit is actually what became brand new. As that experience took place, the Holy Spirit came to live in you. The Holy Spirit is always in communication with the Father and that is how you can pray without ceasing. Your spirit is always in direct connection with the Holy One of Israel. There are definitely times that we need to stop and have a one on one with our Heavenly Father and there are times that we are praying and do not even realize it. Prayer is an enjoyable thing. We don't have to pray but we get to. If you would just think about it for a moment, the Creator of the Universe invites us to have communion with Him. It really is the same as having a conversation with your friend. Prayer is meant to be two-sided, with one talking and the other listening and then the first one listens while the other talks. Prayer should not be a thing to dread but an opportunity to get one step closer to our Lord and Savior. If Jesus needed to take time off and spend it with the Father, how much more do we need that time? As we enter into His presence we find it easier to worship Him. This past week has been an absolutely wonderful week for me. I have gotten up out of bed even earlier than usual and made my way outside to watch the sunrise. As I've watched the world wake up, I have felt the presence of the Lord as I've watched in wonder at one of His wonderful creations. To me, there is no better way to start the day than outside in sweet communion with Him as the daybreaks. I have had plenty of opportunities to get frustrated this week but I have had a deeper peace than in a long time and I know that it is attributed to the time I have spent with Jesus in the morning. You see, worship does not always have to be a loud boisterous occasion; it is taking in the pleasures of life and recognizing that God is the Creator of all things. Since I have given my life to Jesus, I have been a worshipper. I love to sing praises unto my God. I love to just sit in His presence and lavish my love on Him. Some people that know me think that I am just loud and outgoing in my worship. But those that really know me know my quiet side of worshiping the Lord. There are times that I can do nothing but cry in His presence and that is ok. Let me encourage you to become a worshiper and to take time every day to spend in fellowship with the Lord Jesus Christ. It is not necessarily how much time you spend with Him but how you spend time with Him. Are you giving Him yourself (your undivided attention) in prayer or are you always busy doing other things while trying to spend time with Him? There really is nothing better than one on one alone time with our Lord and Savior Jesus Christ.

Thessalonians 5:17 (AMP); Psalm 34:1

Truth to Speak Over Yourself

"No weapon that is formed against me shall prosper, but every tongue that rises against me in judgment, I shall show to be in the wrong."

Devotion:

I don't know about you but there have been times in my walk with the Lord that it has seemed as if all hell has broken loose against me. I have had people come against me, even those that claimed to be my friend. I have had people lie on me, gossip about me, and just flat out be mean to me. But....Jesus! When He was lied on, gossiped about, and people treated Him horribly, He never spoke a word in His defense. He knew that His Father would defend Him. And the good news is that we have the same Father. Isaiah 54:17 (AMP) tells us, "But no weapon that is formed against you shall prosper, and every tongue that shall rise against you in judgment you shall show to be in the wrong. This [peace, righteousness, security, triumph over opposition] is the heritage of the servants of the Lord [those in whom the ideal Servant of the Lord is reproduced]; this is the righteousness *or* the vindication which they obtain from Me [this is that which I impart to them as their justification] says the Lord." Hallelujah! There is nothing that I have to do; all has already been done for me. In the verse above, we read that peace, righteousness, security, and triumph over opposition are the heritage of those that the ideal Servant of the Lord is reproduced in. What are you producing in your life? When we allow Jesus to live His life out in us, to think His thoughts in us, and to walk His life out in us, we are reproducing Him. As we allow Him to flow in us and through us, we will have peace, righteousness, security and triumph over opposition. Jesus had all of the above mentioned in His life and since we are His abiding place, we can have all those in our life, if we allow Him to have His way and not our way. How can we triumph over opposition? The answer might surprise you, by being like Jesus. As we walk in love, grace, mercy, and joy, those that have risen up against us will see Jesus and we will show them to be in the wrong. It's not what we say or do to them but how we live our lives day in and day out. When we do not retaliate against them but love them, they will eventually see the truth and desire it for their own lives. Remember this promise, no weapon that is formed against you shall prosper. Pray for the destruction of all weapons that are sent against you and continue to be all that God wants you to be and you shall triumph victoriously.

Isaiah 54:17 (AMP)

Truth to Speak Over Yourself

"I walk humbly before the Lord that I may receive grace."

Devotion:

"Therefore humble yourselves under the mighty hand of God, that He may exalt you in due time". There have been times in my life that I really wanted a promotion or to get a position that went to someone else. Have you ever been there? I'm sure you have. But I waited my turn. As my husband and I are waiting for doors of ministry to open up for us, we have at times gotten disappointed or discouraged but we will continue to wait on the Lord to open those doors. We will serve in whatever capacity He wants us to serve in. We have helped in areas that were not our 'call' but every child of God is called to SERVE! We can do like many others have done and try to promote ourselves and boast in our abilities or accomplishments but where would that get us? "God resists the proud but gives grace to the humble." I sure do not want God to resist me. I love having open fellowship with Him. We just read in 1 Peter 5:6 that if we will humble ourselves under the mighty hand of God, He will exalt us in due time. I know, I know, God does not work on our timetable. But, God really does know best. We only see what's in front of us and He sees the end. I have thanked God that there were things that He did not allow me to do because in retrospect, I would have ended up hurt. What exactly does it mean to humble ourselves? In the Greek we see that it means base, cast down, humble, of low degree (estate), lowly, abase or bring low. Which in a nutshell means, recognize how big and awesome our God is and how lowly we are in comparison to Him. We have been given power and authority but He has <u>all</u> power and authority. He knows all, sees all, and is in control of absolutely everything. Sometimes we act like we are in control and that we are on the throne dictating what is going to happen in our lives when in actuality it is God Almighty that is on The Throne and it is He that is in control. We cannot dare to try and tell Him what to do although at times we try. It is at those times in our lives that He will resist us. Only when we come to Him in total surrender and admit our helplessness without His help will He exalt us. Why don't we go to the foot of the Cross together right now and bring ourselves low at the feet of Jesus and let Him be the one who exalts us in due time, the time that He knows we can handle the promotion and not succumb to pride?

1 Peter 5:5b-6 (Greek meanings taken from the Strong's Exhaustive Concordance)

Truth to Speak Over Yourself

"I acknowledge the Lord in all my ways, therefore, He directs my path."

Devotion:

"In all your ways know, recognize, *and* acknowledge Him, and He will direct *and* make straight *and* plain your paths." Have you ever wondered, "What am I meant to do?" or "Is this what You want me to do Lord?" The verse that we just read says that if we will know, recognize, and acknowledge the Lord in all of our ways, He will direct and make straight and plain our paths. Most mornings when I start my day, I invite Jesus to live His life out through me, think His thoughts in me, and walk His life out in me. When I do this, I am acknowledging Him in all my ways. Now, don't get me wrong, there have been times that I have been led astray by my own desires that had nothing to do with the Lord but those times are getting fewer and farther in between. I have come to a place in my walk with the Lord that I recognize that absolutely nothing comes into my life without His first knowing about it. Everything that happens in my life had to come through Him first. After all, He is the Omniscient One, the All-knowing One. Just as Satan had to get permission from God to try to bring Job down and he had to get permission from Jesus to sift Peter like wheat, he has to get permission from God to try to take us down. But, we do not have to allow Him to take us down, for we have the Greater One living in us. We have been given all power and authority over the enemy. There are times that we have opened the door for Satan to have legal access in our lives and then we need to be quick to repent and get that door closed fast. God said that He would direct our paths. It is time that we start asking Him first what He wants us to do or where He wants us to go before we already have it settled in our hearts, because then we are really wanting our way and not His. Let me give you an example, a few years back, someone had given me a really nice car and I kept the car for about a year but then I decided that I needed a van. Did you catch the word I in that sentence? So anyhow, I went to see about trading in my car (which was paid for) and getting a loan to buy the van that I wanted. I reasoned that if God did not want me to have the van, I would not get a loan. Well, the car dealer knew his banker really well so guess what? Yep, I got the loan and off the lot I drove with a van that I now owed a lot of money for. And of course, I said that it must have been God's will for me to have the van since I got the loan but I only prayed about it after I already had it settled in my heart that I wanted the van and what a blessing I would be to all the kids that needed a ride to church. I ended up being in debt to that van for three years. God tells us in His Word that we are to owe no man anything except to love him in Christ so it was not God's will for me to buy the van when I already had a perfectly good car that was paid for. I let my own selfish desires get in the way of God directing my paths. I have since repented and He made a way for me to get the van paid for but not before it cost me a whole lot of money for finance charges and repairs. I now trust in Him that He really does know what is best for me and that He will lead me in paths that will cause me to grow and be prosperous. Won't you join me today in inviting Jesus to live His life out through you, think His thoughts in you, and walk His life out in you?

Proverbs 3:6 (AMP); Romans 13:8; Job 1:6-12; Luke 22:31

Truth to Speak Over Yourself

"The joy of the Lord is my strength."

Devotion:

The joy of the Lord is my strength, the joy of the Lord is my strength, the joy of the Lord is my strength, ha, ha, ha, ha, ha. I know you have heard the song that I am attempting to write. Whenever you are having a down moment if you will take the time to sing that song, you will feel your spirits begin to lift and soon you'll find yourself laughing. The joy that I am talking about is not the stuff that we feel when all is going well in our lives, but the sensation in our spirit that all is well, regardless of what is happening. The emotion we feel when all is going well is called happiness. That is based on our happenings or our happenstance. Happiness comes and goes because it is based on temporal things. Joy stays because it is based on what Jesus has done for us and who Jesus is in us. In Nehemiah 8:10 b (AMP) we can read "And be not grieved *and* depressed, for the joy of the Lord is your strength *and* stronghold." Throughout the Word of God we see that we have choices to make and even here we have the choice to either be grieved and depressed or let the joy of the Lord be our strength and stronghold. You may be wondering how do I get the joy of the Lord? Here are two Scriptures that will help you understand; "You have made known to me the ways of life; You will make me full of joy in your presence." And "You will show me the path of life; in Your presence is fullness of joy, at Your right hand there are pleasures forevermore." Do you see any similarity in the above two verses? You got it; we have the joy of the Lord in the very presence of the Lord. Not only do we have joy but the fullness of joy. If we begin to feel depleted in strength it is at that very moment that we need to get into the presence of the Lord and then we will be strengthened and filled with the fullness of joy that we need. Not only do we receive strength and joy but also in His presence, we are shown the path of life. Oh, what benefits we will receive if we only take the time to enter into the presence of the Lord. We will find all the strength, joy, and answers to the decisions we have to make in His presence. There is no better way to live our lives than daily in His presence. May His presence be so manifest in your life today that you will be filled to overflowing with strength and joy.

Nehemiah 8:10b (AMP); Acts 2:28; Psalm 16:11 (AMP)

Truth to Speak Over Yourself

"I am blessed that I can be a blessing to others."

Devotion:

The Lord will never take you where He will not provide for you. Some of the Hebrew meanings for the word blessed are; to kneel; by implication to bless God (as an act of adoration), abundantly, altogether, at all, greatly, indeed, and thank. Some of the meanings in the Greek are as follows: to speak well of, i.e. (religiously) to bless (thank or invoke a benediction upon, prosper), adorable, supremely blessed, well off, fortunate, and happy. Wow, what a mouth full. My family and I are truly blessed. We have accepted the sacrifice of Jesus Christ for the atonement of our sins, sickness, and disease. If God were to do nothing more in our lives, He has already done more than enough. Our desire should be one of Lord, bless me that I may be a blessing to others. It does not matter what things look like to the natural man but the Spirit of God says you are blessed. God has provided for our every need: physical, spiritual, financial, and mental. What more could a person truly ask for? Take the time today to encourage yourself in today's 'truth to speak over yourself'. Regardless of how things appear, all of your household members are blessed. This does not mean that we can go about doing our own thing with no thought of what God would have us to do, but it does help us to realize that when we are walking with Him and allowing Him to walk His life out through us, we are blessed in all our deeds and we are blessed when we come in and when we go out. The closer that I get to Jesus, the more He amazes me with His blessings, and the more I desire to bless God by kneeling down and simply adoring Him.

Deuteronomy 28:6 (Hebrew and Greek meanings taken from the Strong's Exhaustive Concordance)

Truth to Speak Over Yourself

"I delight myself in the Lord; therefore, I will have the desires of my heart."

Devotion:

There is nothing greater than delighting oneself in the Lord. Just when I think that I am so exhausted from the cares of the world, God steps in and refreshes me. As I begin to think on His goodness and His mercy, I find myself smiling and my spirit begins to lift. The desires that are in my heart were actually placed there by Him so of course, He wants me to have those desires fulfilled. One of the lessons that I have learned in my walk with the Lord is that sometimes I must wait. Now, I know that seems like it ought to be a word we should abstain from saying but God does tell us, "those that wait upon the Lord, shall renew their strength." As I wait for my desires to be manifest, my strength is being renewed. Isn't that awesome? Not only will my desires be fulfilled but my strength gets renewed too. What an awesome God we serve. There is a very special person in my life that I have not spoken to in 13 years and I finally found him and we have been in contact with one another. God knew that this was a top priority desire and it has been fulfilled. Well, partially anyhow. As of right now we've only been in contact via email but by the time this is published, I believe that we will have seen each other again face to face. I want to get back to the real key in having the desires of our heart met. It is found in delighting ourselves in the Lord. We have all kinds of activities in our lives and things that we really enjoy doing, like watching television, watching sports, reading books, talking on the telephone, eating chocolate, or being on the computer, just to mention a few examples, but the One that we should delight ourselves in is our Lord and Savior Jesus Christ. He loves to have us spend time with Him just as much as we love to spend time with Him. I love spending time with my husband but even that does not compare to spending intimate quality time with my Jesus. He touches my spirit in a way that no person can ever touch me. It is great to have people in our lives that we can share our ups and downs with but the One who is the answer is Jesus. It is Him whom I really delight in spending time with. Sometimes I'm considered unfriendly because I would much rather be alone with Jesus than with other people. But Jesus is the One who saved me, delivered me, healed me, and filled me with the Holy Ghost. He is the One who deserves my attention more than the others do. I'm not talking about locking yourself in your home and never coming out or talking to other people, just remember he is Number One. He is the One that knows me and understands me like no one else and the best part is He loves me just the same. I would like to encourage you today to put down the remote, close the blinds, and start delighting yourself in the Lord and watch the desires of your heart become a reality in the here and now.

Psalm 37:4; Isaiah 40:31

Closing word from Lori:

It has been such a joy to my heart to share all these Truths to Speak Over Yourself with you. All the promises in the Word of God are ours for the taking if we will only ask and believe. We are told that "faith comes by hearing and hearing by the Word" so it has been my prayer that as you have read and heard the Word, your faith has been expanded. If you would allow me to pray one more time for you:

Father God, I love You and adore You. I am so thankful for all that You have accomplished in the lives of those that have read the words written in Truths To Speak Over Yourself. Holy Spirit, I ask that You would take the words that they have heard and plant them deep within their spirit. Let the words grow and bring forth much fruit in their lives. I pray that everything that may hinder them from fulfilling Your promises for their lives would be made null and void right now in Jesus name. Bring forth a renewed hunger and passion for the things of God. Let their hope be restored. I thank You Jesus that You have made a way where there seems to be no way. I ask that everyone that comes into contact with this book would find the Truth for his or her soul. I give You praise, glory and honor. In Jesus name, Amen and Amen.

Update: My son Brian and I were reacquainted in March of 2009. We have begun developing a fantastic relationship. Please be encouraged, the Lord does hear and answer prayer.

Be blessed my new friends. Continue to enjoy this journey that you are on with Jesus Christ.

Rev. Lori Skipper

About The Author:

Lori Skipper is a called Prophet of God for these end times. Since accepting Jesus Christ as her personal Lord and Savior, she has been ministering the Word of God throughout Southern Illinois, Central Illinois, Eastern Missouri, and Southeastern Oklahoma. She has been given a call to "preach and teach the unadulterated truth of the Word of God" and she does just that.

Lori started her evangelistic ministry in 1999. She was Interim Pastor at Iuka United Pentecostal Church in Iuka, Illinois in 2003. Lori lives with her husband in Palmetto, FL.

For more information, or to schedule Lori Skipper for a speaking engagement, please write to:

                Lori Skipper
          900 9th Ave E Lot 211
           Palmetto, FL 34221
             813-481-5751

E-mail: lorilyn1985@gmail.com